EAST CAROLINA UNIVERSITY FOOTBALL

Head coach Clarence Stasavich shares a new piece of safety equipment with players and coaches in the locker room of Christenbury Memorial Gymnasium. At far right is Odell Welborn, who coached the East Carolina linemen and taught at the local high school, J.H. Rose, in Greenville. (Courtesy of East Carolina University Archives.)

FRONT COVER: Dave Bumgarner (No. 87) and Bill Cline (No. 43) celebrate the Pirates' victory in the 1964 Tangerine Bowl. The pair combined to lead the Pirates to an 18-1 run beginning with a September 21, 1963, win over Wake Forest University. Both were later inducted into the East Carolina University Athletics Hall of Fame. (Courtesy of East Carolina University Archives.)

FRONT COVER BACKGROUND: East Carolina fans cheer on the Pirates in Dowdy-Ficklen Stadium. Originally known as Ficklen Stadium, alumni Ron and Mary Ellen Dowdy donated more than $1 million in 1994 during a stadium renovation campaign. To honor the gift, the stadium was renamed Dowdy-Ficklen Stadium. (Courtesy of East Carolina University Archives.)

BACK COVER: Chancellor Leo Jenkins raises a finger and Coach Pat Dye enjoys a cigar in the locker room as the Pirates celebrate winning the Southern Conference championship in 1976. It was East Carolina's last Southern Conference title; the Pirates returned to independent status in 1977. (Courtesy of East Carolina University Archives.)

EAST CAROLINA UNIVERSITY FOOTBALL

Arthur Carlson, Elizabeth Brooke Tolar, and John Allen Tucker

ARCADIA PUBLISHING

ISBN 978-1-4671-1645-9

Published by Arcadia Publishing
Charleston, South Carolina

Printed in the United States of America

Library of Congress Control Number: 2015954833

For all general information, please contact Arcadia Publishing:
Telephone 843-853-2070
Fax 843-853-0044
E-mail sales@arcadiapublishing.com
For customer service and orders:
Toll-Free 1-888-313-2665

Visit us on the Internet at www.arcadiapublishing.com

Dedicated to Hayley Carlson, Kate and Kaleigh Tucker, and A.J. Maxey.

CONTENTS

ACKNOWLEDGMENTS

A work of this nature is impossible without the aid of many contributors and, moreover, a community of supportive individuals united in their passion for East Carolina University athletics. Foremost among them are the Pirate fans, players, coaches, and athletics staff members who have contributed to the football program since 1932. This work would also not have been possible without the generous support of so many at East Carolina, notably Chancellor Steve Ballard, Provost Ron Mitchelson, Joyner Library director Jan Lewis, athletics director Jeff Compher, and assistant athletics director for media Tom McClellan. A special thanks to our editor at Arcadia, Liz Gurley, who always kept us on task and offered words of support and professional encouragement throughout the process.

We also owe a debt of gratitude to our colleagues in Joyner Library, particularly the staff of the University Archives; the Digital Collections team; and the Department of Athletics. We are equally grateful for the kind assistance of the Department of Athletics, the Pirate Club, and those many others who have worked to document the rich history of Pirate football, including Henry Ferrell, William Ritenour, Mary Jo Jackson Bratton, James Batten, the successive editors of East Carolina yearbooks—the *Tecoan* and the *Buccaneer*—as well as numerous sports writers for the Greenville *Daily Reflector* and our campus newspaper, *The East Carolinian*. Also, we would like to thank the many alumni, staff, and friends who shared their own memories of Pirate football.

Without exception, all images appearing in this book are from the holdings of the East Carolina University Archives or the East Carolina University Department of Athletics.

INTRODUCTION

East Carolina University (ECU) football traces its beginnings to the administration of Robert H. Wright, the school's first president. As an undergraduate, Wright served as captain of the football team at the University of North Carolina at Chapel Hill. Yet with an overwhelmingly female campus at East Carolina, President Wright had to wait until the 1930s, when men began enrolling in significant numbers, to oversee the emergence of East Carolina football. In 1932, two years before Wright's 25th year as president, the first men's football team took the field. Wright's consistent support for physical fitness, intramural sports, and finally, intercollegiate football, set the tone for much that would follow.

Early on, the team was known as the "Teachers," reflecting the school's charter mission of teacher training. The team practiced on the east end of campus. Early pictures feature the distinctive architecture of the Model School (now Messick Theater Arts Building) in the background. Lacking bleachers, spectators stood along the sidelines to cheer on the Teachers. Games were initially played off-campus, at Guy Smith Stadium. In 1949, College Stadium, on the southeast end of campus, became the new venue for Pirate football.

With increased male enrollment and the resulting transformation of campus culture, the Teacher name was revisited: noting that the pirate Blackbeard was supposedly named Edward Teach, campus historians punned that the Teachers might be the Pirates, with none other than Blackbeard as their mascot. The 1934 yearbook, the *Tecoan*, illustrated this new identity with cartoon figures depicting buccaneers, pirate ships, and buried treasure juxtaposed with images of campus culture. By the early 1950s, the team and the campus had embraced the pirate image as their own.

Pirate momentum halted during World War II due to wartime exigencies. Just prior to the war, Coach John Christenbury led the 1940 team to an unprecedented 6-2 season. The next year, East Carolina went undefeated in seven games, a unique achievement in Pirate football history. Christenbury enlisted to serve his country, but died tragically in an accidental explosion at Port Chicago, California, in 1944. Due to his team's historic achievement in 1941 and his outstanding contributions to Pirate football, the new gymnasium on the east end of campus was named for him in 1953. Forty years later, Christenbury was inducted into the ECU Athletics Hall of Fame.

The GI Bill made higher education possible for many veterans, as well as those who served in the years following World War II. Many chose to study at East Carolina, which remained largely female in 1945. Football returned in 1946, and a succession of solid seasons ensued. In 1952, Coach Jack Boone led the team to its first bowl game. While the Pirates lost to Clarion College in the Lion's Bowl, the achievement set a new standard for athletic success at East Carolina.

In the postwar years, the football team advanced the pirate identity on the field as well as on campus. The 1952 *Tecoan* contributed to this with a cover featuring a peg-legged buccaneer standing on a treasure chest, with a skull-and-crossbones flag behind him. Homecoming parades featured floats with maritime themes and coeds wearing pirate boots. In 1953, a sword-brandishing swashbuckler again graced the front cover of the yearbook, now renamed the *Buccaneer*.

By 1960, East Carolina had grown from a teacher training school into a teacher's college, and then from a teacher's college into a liberal arts college. In the 1960s, phenomenal growth continued, culminating in the school's attainment of university status in 1967. Along with increased enrollment and the development of diverse graduate programs came the expansion of the athletic complex, now moved from the east end of campus up College Hill and across 14th Street. This new stadium was originally named James S. Ficklen Memorial Stadium (1963–1994). New leadership appeared with Clarence Stasavich, who served as head coach from 1962 to 1969. During the Stasavich era, the Pirates achieved an outstanding 50-27-1 record and successive bowl game invitations. In 1963, the Pirates won their first bowl game with a victory over Northeastern in the Eastern Bowl. In 1964, the team won another bowl game, against the University of Massachusetts. In 1965, the Pirates racked up yet another bowl victory, this time against Maine in the Tangerine Bowl. In 1966, Stasavich led the Pirates, new to the Southern Conference as of 1965, to a conference championship, their first in 13 years.

Pirate football in the 1970s featured a succession of coaches including Mike McGee (1970), Sonny Randle (1971–1973), and Pat Dye (1974–1979). Dye emerged as the most successful coach in Pirate history, achieving an overall record of 48-18-1, along with a Southern Conference championship in 1976. In 1977, Dye led the Pirates to victories against in-state rivals NC State (28-23) and Duke (17-16). In 1978, the Pirates defeated Louisiana Tech in the Independence Bowl. Following the 1979 season, Dye left East Carolina to become head coach at Wyoming before moving to Auburn in 1981. He was inducted into the ECU Athletics Hall of Fame in 2006.

The 1980s was not the best of decades for the Pirates: apart from the 1983 season, during which the team achieved an 8-3 record and national ranking, there were no winning records, and certainly no bowl games. Bill Lewis's tenure as head coach (1989–1991) did include, however, an impressive winning season (11-1) in 1991, a Peach Bowl win over rival NC State University, and national ranking. Although Lewis left to serve as head coach for Georgia Tech the same year, into the vacuum came Steve Logan, who led the Pirates to an unbroken record for total wins (69-58), plus five bowl game appearances from 1992 to 2002. Following a poor season in 2002, Logan left East Carolina. Undoubtedly, he was one of the most successful Pirate coaches in school history.

The Pirates did not regain momentum until the 2005 season under Skip Holtz, who led the team to a memorable victory against Duke (24-21) in his first home game. In the years that followed, the Pirates returned to winning seasons and successive bowl game appearances. Moreover, the Pirates won Conference USA championships in 2008 and again in 2009. Holtz left ECU after the 2009 season, moving to the University of South Florida.

Former ECU defensive back Ruffin McNeill followed Holtz as the Pirates' head coach in 2010. McNeil's best seasons were in 2012 (8-5) and 2013 (10-3). The 2013 season was most memorable for East Carolina's commanding victories over UNC-Chapel Hill (55-31) in Dowdy-Ficklen Stadium, and over NC State University (42-28) at Carter-Finley Stadium in Raleigh. Although McNeill led the Pirates to three bowl games in a row, following the 2015 season, when the team ended with a losing record and no bowl invitations, he was relieved of his duties as head coach. On December 13, 2015, East Carolina announced it had hired Scotty Montgomery as its new head football coach. A North Carolina native, Montgomery served as the offensive coordinator at Duke University as well as the wide receivers coach for the Pittsburgh Steelers.

Today, Pirate football is more important than ever, having become a key unifying force of campus culture, bringing together disparate fields and disciplines in support of the athletic expression of the school's identity. With generous leadership and relentless service from the Pirate Club, Pirate football and ECU athletics have repeatedly advanced to the next level of excellence on the field and in service to the region. Having known considerable greatness, Pirate fans now expect nothing less.

1

The Origins of Football at East Carolina

In 1907, the North Carolina General Assembly chartered East Carolina Teachers Training School to train young men and women professionally to become teachers. Although the school opened in 1909, men did not begin enrolling for the normal school program until 1932. Pictured here is Old Austin, the school's original administrative and classroom building. Razed in 1968, Old Austin lives on by way of a larger-scale replica of its distinctive cupola located on the campus mall.

Pictured here is East Carolina's first president, Robert Herring Wright (1870–1934). While a student at the University of North Carolina–Chapel Hill, Wright captained the football and track teams. Throughout his tenure at East Carolina, he stressed physical fitness and implemented a mandatory physical activity program centered primarily on basketball and tennis.

Before East Carolina participated in intercollegiate athletics, all-girls' basketball teams were organized on campus and competed on outdoor courts for bragging rights. Each school year's top basketball squad was celebrated and its accomplishment etched on a trophy to be passed down to the next year's winners. Here, Prof. Herbert Austin poses with the triumphant class of 1915 squad.

Victorious members of the class of 1930 pose with their hard-earned trophy. The most dominant of the intramural teams, these ladies won three consecutive campus championships. They were led by Jane Gold Hardee of Greenville (seated on the ball). The trophy is currently housed in the East Carolina University Archives.

The arrival of a fair number of male students at East Carolina in 1932 resulted in many changes on campus. Among the most noteworthy was the implementation of intercollegiate athletics. Here, members of East Carolina's first football team pose for their yearbook photograph. Despite coach Charles "Kenneth" Beatty's efforts, the Teachers failed to score a single point in five contests and ended the year without a win. During their first season, the team only played two home games, one against Guilford College on November 12, 1932, and another against the NC State University freshman team the following Saturday.

Pictured in this 1964 photograph is Charles "Kenneth" Beatty. A native of Mount Holly, North Carolina, Beatty attended NC State University and Guilford College, where he participated in baseball and football. He eventually joined the North Carolina National Guard, which brought him to Greenville, where he worked with the local high school football team. He was only 28 when he agreed in 1932 to serve as the volunteer coach of the East Carolina program. Beatty resigned after the 1933 campaign with a record of 1-10. In 1974, a year after his death, he was inducted into the ECU Athletics Hall of Fame. Beatty Street in Greenville is named in his honor.

With Beatty's resignation, Athletics Council chair Ralph Deal selected Graham "Doc" Mathis (1909–1986) as East Carolina's new coach. An accomplished athlete at Davidson College, the 24-year-old Mathis remains the youngest coach in East Carolina history. Drawing an annual salary of $350, Mathis was also the first paid coach at East Carolina.

Despite little success in the early years, support for Pirate football was fervent from the beginning. While the small number of enrolled males was reflected on the depth chart, the composition of the student body, along with reduced competition for playing time in the 1930s, prompted many men to enroll at East Carolina instead of other institutions.

With increased male enrollment, Doc Mathis was able to properly align talent with positions. Despite the increased talent and East Carolina's transition from a teachers' training school into an official college, the football team still played its home games on a field of grass near the campus vegetable garden. Wright Field, as the area was known, now houses the Austin Building. Before small but enthusiastic crowds, Mathis's squads were noted for adding an aerial component to their offense. On November 11, 1934, the Pirates hosted their first out-of-state opponent, the Norfolk campus of William and Mary College, now Old Dominion University. The game ended in a 0-0 tie. A loss the next week to Lenoir-Rhyne ended Mathis's first season as coach with a record of 1-4-1. Mathis resigned after his second year, eventually landing at Elon College as athletics director. In 1979, he was inducted into the Elon Athletics Hall of Fame.

Originally East Carolina's sports teams competed under the moniker of "Teachers," as a nod to their intended profession. Seeking something more intimidating, many of the students drew upon the similarity between the word "teacher" and "Teach," the supposed last name of the notorious pirate Blackbeard, whose home was just east of Greenville in Bath, North Carolina. In 1934, the yearbook was rife with pirate-themed imagery. Previous themes included Shakespearean drama, the Old South, and futurism, giving rise to speculation on what mascots selected from those genres might have been. During the 1935 season, news outlets regularly referred to the "Pirates" of East Carolina in their sports pages.

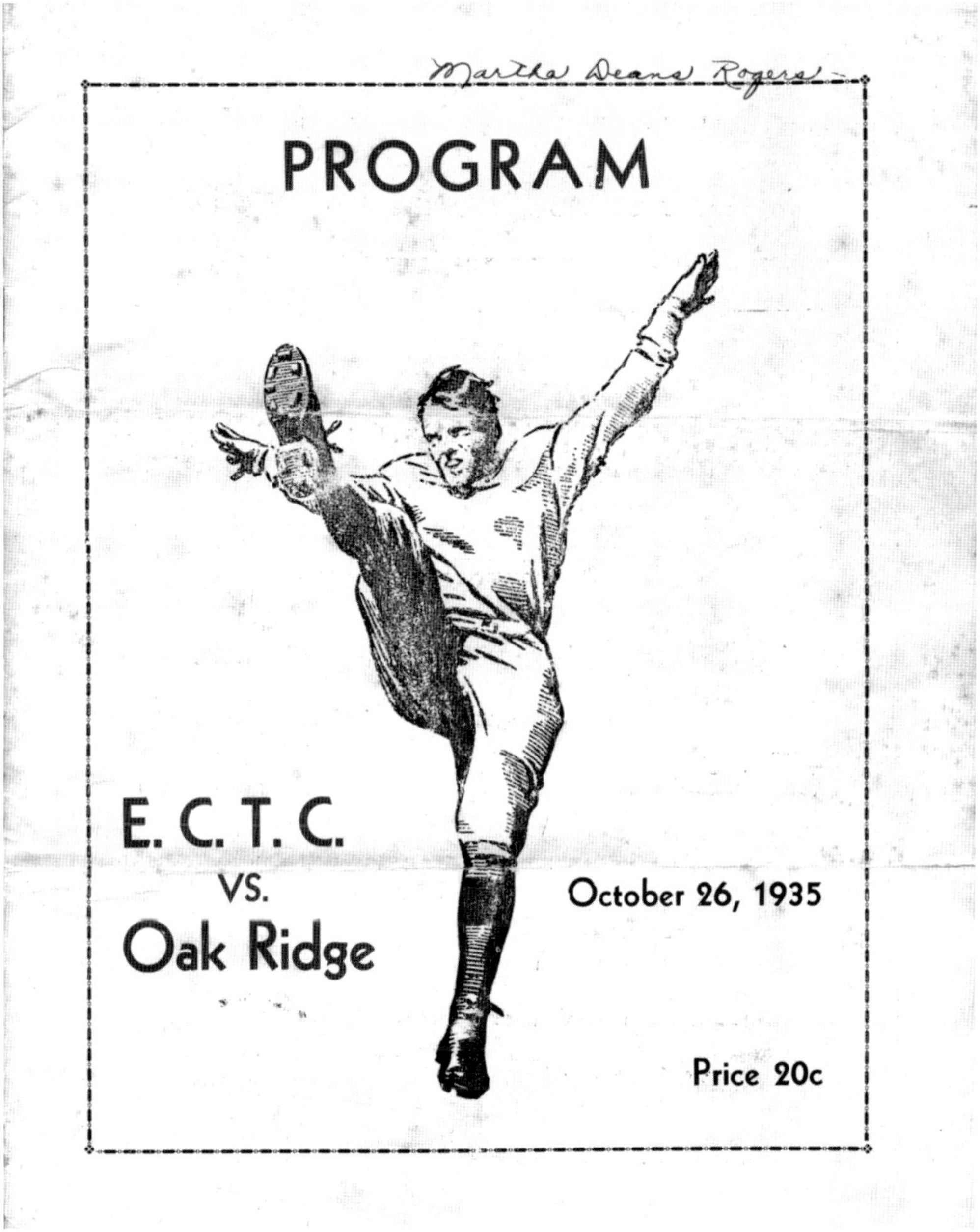

By 1935, football games were among the premier events hosted on campus. Game-day programs, like the one shown here, provided fans with facts about each squad. On this day, the Pirates lost 6-2 with a late safety accounting for their only score and the first points of the season. Often physically outmatched but indomitable in spirit, the 23 active members of the 1935 Pirate football team averaged just 167 pounds. A season-ending 13-0 shutout victory over Louisburg College left the 1935 team with a .500 record and, most notably, its first non-losing season. The 20¢ price on this earliest surviving program available for East Carolina football was a relative bargain even for 1935.

Roland "Bo" Farley (1907–1999), a former professional baseball player for the St. Louis Cardinals, led the 1936 football squad. During his time at Duke as a three-sport star, he played for both Wallace Wade and Eddie Cameron. The 26-year-old Farley was a player-coach at East Carolina, earning his education degree in 1939. Despite leading the Pirates to their first winning season, Farley did not return as a football coach after graduating. He did, however, continue coaching basketball and baseball for East Carolina.

On November 21, 1936, East Carolina played its first homecoming game against Louisburg College. An estimated 1,500 fans attended the season-ending affair. The 19-0 Pirate victory capped off a 3-2 season.

This is the earliest football action shot available in the East Carolina University Archives. The Pirates compete against an unidentified opponent on a section of campus known as Wright Field near the modern-day Austin Building. The Model School, now the Messick Theater Arts Building, is in the background.

The year 1937 was one of change for Pirate football, beginning with the introduction of new athletic director and head coach Joseph D. "Swede" Alexander. Coached by the legendary Glenn "Pop" Warner during his time at Iowa State, Alexander was warmly received by the student body.

The introduction of the classification system in college football marked another major change for the Pirates. The National Collegiate Athletic Association (NCAA) classified schools with football teams into three tiers: major colleges, small colleges, and no classification. The Pirates were designated a small college program.

Hopeful for a breakout year, Coach Alexander entered the 1938 season with only nine returning lettermen. His optimism was short-lived, however, as the Pirates lost the first two games by a combined margin of 38-6. A 7-6 victory over Western Carolina was the Pirates' only win of the season, though they managed a 7-7 tie against their rival, Guilford College. In the spring of 1939, Alexander resigned and returned to his native Texas.

Despite beliefs that the 1939 squad represented the best prospective team in school history, the Pirates were beset with injuries, losing two returning starters before the first game was played. A string of dismal losses sapped the popularity of the football team, with basketball and baseball drawing larger crowds.

Oscar A. "Hank" Hanker served as the fifth head football coach at East Carolina. A graduate of the University of Illinois, Hanker only coached a single season. He nonetheless advanced Pirate football with his choice of successor.

As successor to Coach Hanker, John Christenbury (1907–1944) inherited a demoralized squad. Born in Charlotte, North Carolina, Christenbury attended Davidson College, where he was a three-sport letterman for the Wildcats and a teammate of "Doc" Mathis. In 1940, Christenbury left his position at Brevard College to teach physical education and coach football at East Carolina. As a testament to the loyalty he garnered, 17 of his Brevard players followed him to Greenville. Although fewer than 300 men were enrolled at East Carolina, Christenbury began recruiting for the Pirates. His personality and growing reputation helped him attract athletes from across the state. A strict disciplinarian, Christenbury imposed a firm set of rules on the 1940 team. In addition to the normal rules involving class attendance and minimum grade requirements, he banned smoking, alcohol, and dating in-season.

Deploying the single-wing formation common to the era, Christenbury was able to field a squad with appropriately skilled starters and backups in 1940. The first game of the Christenbury era was a 14-6 victory over Kutztown State. The second game of the season featured another Pirate first—an estimated 2,000 fans watched the Pirates play their first night game, a drubbing of the Presbyterian Junior College Scots, under the lights at Greenville's Guy Smith Stadium, approximately three miles from campus. At the end of the season, the Pirates' record of 5-3 reignited football fever on campus, a fervor that would only be interrupted by World War II.

Established in 1933, the Varsity Club at East Carolina was composed of lettermen in football, basketball, baseball, and tennis. The club assisted with fundraising, enhancing campus physical activity offerings, and fostering a cooperative attitude among the athletes of the various teams. As a nod to East Carolina's roots, the Varsity Club sweater worn by these 1940 members features a large "T" in honor of their beginnings as the Teachers.

The Pirates' Billy Greene (No. 21, at left in dark top) blocks a punt during the second quarter against Western Carolina. Avenging a loss in Cullowhee the previous year, East Carolina emerged victorious with a score of 19-6. The Catamounts were a regular fixture on the Pirates' schedule until the early 1960s.

Offensive lineman Bill Lucas demonstrates proper technique for his teammates as he attacks a blocking dummy. Multiple opponents complimented the hard-nosed Pirates as the hardest hitting team on their schedules.

Christenbury realized that technique was essential to overcoming physical limitations, particularly when playing established programs. Focusing on fundamentals, "Honest John," as his players called him, conducted practices that featured both physical drills and the use of classroom sessions to emphasize the intricacies of strategy. In this image, two of his offensive lineman, tackle James Little (left) and guard Bill Lucas, race toward the camera as if preparing to clear a running lane.

In 1941, the Pirates introduced a new uniform befitting a program on the rise. Some accounts lamented that the previous gold uniforms with purple trim had faded to mustard yellow. Primarily purple with gold accents, the new design was personally influenced by Christenbury. These uniforms also included the adoption of the modern-style plastic helmet, though budget concerns limited their availability to select team members. With the World War II draft already drawing men away from campuses nationwide, the Pirates were forced to add non-college teams to their schedule as replacements for shuttered programs. Several, such as the Norfolk Naval Air Station team, featured former professional players since they were not bound by NCAA eligibility rules.

Members of the 1941 Pirate team prepare for another grueling practice session. Their dedication would pay dividends that year as they finished the season with a perfect 7-0, the only undefeated, untied season in school history. Led by a dominating defense that forced four shutouts, East Carolina cumulatively outscored their opponents by a margin of 159-20. There was little jubilation on the ride home from the season-ending game against Belmont Abbey in Gastonia, however, as the East Carolina players passed numerous military installations in North Carolina. Soon, the horrors of a country at war would touch the most unlikely among them.

After the Japanese attack on Pearl Harbor in 1941, travel restrictions and the continued loss of men to military service forced many schools to suspend their intercollegiate athletics programs. School president Leon Meadows followed the lead of other institutions and cancelled the 1942 football season. East Carolina did not play another game until 1946, after the end of World War II. In 1943, Christenbury volunteered for the US Naval Reserves. He was assigned duties as a munitions loading officer, stationed at Port Chicago, California.

On July 17, 1944, Port Chicago was rocked by an explosion felt more than 500 miles away. Two ships collided, igniting an eruption that claimed 320 lives, including that of John Christenbury. East Carolina's new gym, completed in 1953, was dedicated in his memory.

2

The Return of Pirate Football

Thanks to the GI Bill, men leaving military service began enrolling at East Carolina in greater numbers after World War II. An Athletic Finance Committee supported a newly founded Athletic Council. Thanks to the backing of successive East Carolina presidents, Dr. Howard McGinnis and Dr. Dennis Cooke, the Pirates would soon be ready to take to the field once more.

The ECU Athletics Department needed new leadership in 1946. John Christenbury's death, Hank Hankers's retirement for medical reasons, and Ralph Deal's mandatory retirement at the age of 65 forced East Carolina to choose a new chairman of athletics. Dennis Cooke selected psychology professor Dr. Carl Adams (left) for this role. As the faculty advisor to the Veteran's Club, Adams was acquainted with a surplus of men willing to play football. Cooke just needed to find a coach.

Adams selected James "Big Jim" Johnson (1912–2004) as the next Pirate football coach. A 1937 graduate of East Carolina Teachers College, Johnson was a natural leader and a three-sport athlete for the Pirates. He served as captain of the football, basketball, and baseball teams during his playing days. As coach and chairman of the athletics committee, Johnson resolved to restore Pirate athletics despite the lack of available scholarships, assistant coaches, and scouting. Johnson resigned after the 1948 season with a record of 8-18-1. A lifelong Pirate, he was instrumental in the founding of the East Carolina Educational Foundation (Pirate Club) and was inducted into the ECU Athletics Hall of Fame in 1978.

The members of the 1946 football team pose on campus near Wright Field. The first game of the season, which happened to be the first game in four years, took place in Maxton, North Carolina, against Presbyterian Junior College. Behind a stout offensive line, the Pirates rolled to a 39-0 shutout victory, marking a triumphant return for Pirate football. The team finished the season 5-3-1 with all three losses to North State Conference opponents—Elon, Western Carolina, and Lenoir-Rhyne. The Pirate victories included triumphs over Erksine, Newport News Apprentice Academy, Atlantic Christian, and Fort Bragg. Playing Atlantic Christian twice was necessary owing to scheduling difficulties caused by East Carolina's lack of conference affiliation.

The Pirates continued to host many of their games in Guy Smith Stadium. The distinctive cover for the stands is evident on the right side of this image and is still visible to those traveling along Moye Boulevard or Memorial Drive today.

Dennis Cooke (1904–1982) only served as East Carolina's president for one year but was instrumental in restarting the football program after World War II. He believed that "a fine school spirit and an adequate and comprehensive athletic program is indispensable." Cooke left East Carolina to serve as president at High Point College from 1947 to 1959.

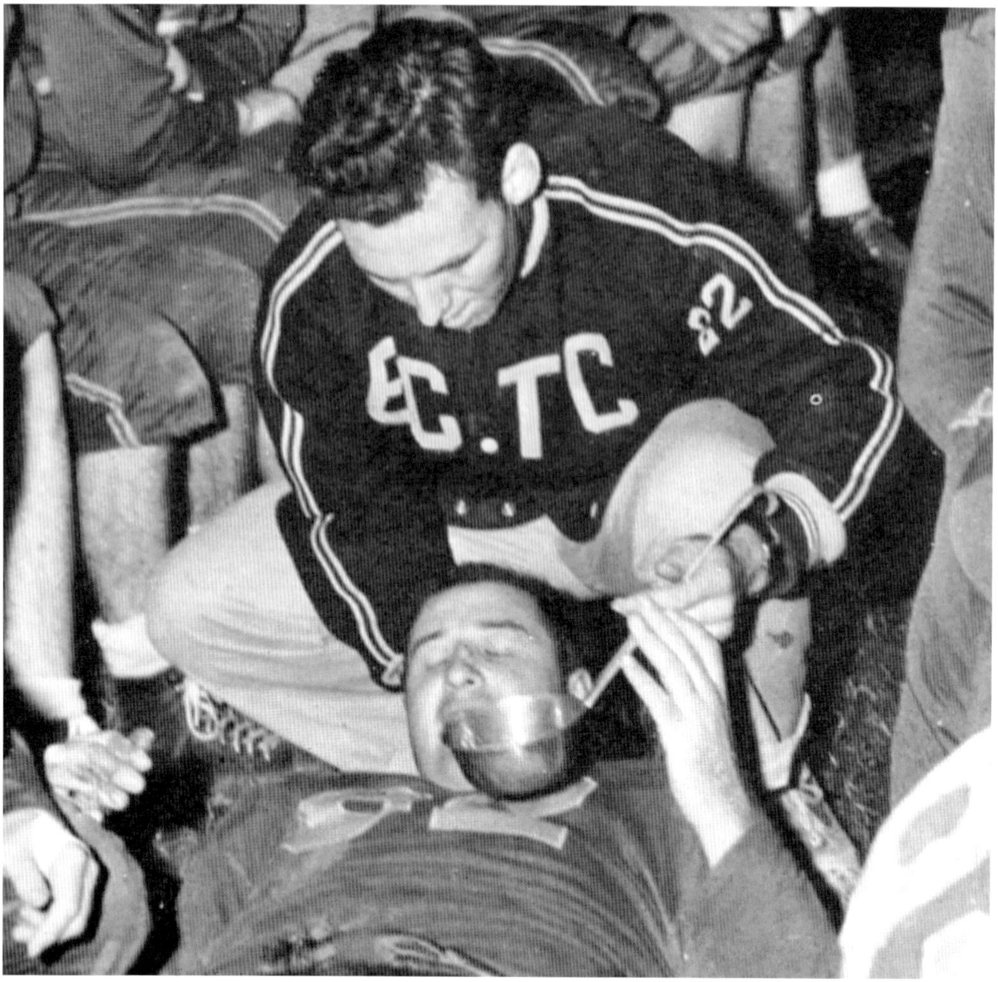

In 1947, eighty eligible students attended football tryouts, the largest turnout in school history. In another historic milestone, the Pirates were set to play in the North State Conference as provisional members. Formed in 1929, the conference included teams from the Piedmont and western areas of North Carolina, such as Catawba, Elon, Lenoir-Rhyne, and Western Carolina. The excitement over admission into the North State Conference following a winning campaign the previous year may have been too much for this Pirate to overcome, as a teammate had to assist him with a ladle of water.

Admission into the North State Conference did include drawbacks. Many of East Carolina's recent transfers were declared ineligible owing to conference rules. Coach Johnson was prepared for this development and recruited potential freshmen with the promise of playing time. Among them was prized fullback recruit Jimmy Smith of Portsmouth, Virginia. Smith combined with Franz Holscher, Allen Barry, Frank Meannle, and Roger Thrift to form a deep backfield to execute Coach Johnson's heavy run-based attack.

Head coach Jim Johnson (second from left) confers with his assistants Ellie Fearing (far left), Howard Porter (second from right), and Pete Everett (far right) as they discuss strategy during a break in practice. After his playing days at East Carolina under "Doc" Mathis, Johnson entered the US Navy as a combat aviator. While in the Navy, he played on a service football team under the direction of College Football Hall of Fame inductee Don Faurot. Faurot was instrumental in teaching Johnson the Split-T formation. This formation proved popular with Faurot's protégés, Jim Tatum and Charles "Bud" Wilkerson, as well.

John Decatur Messick accepted the post of East Carolina president after the departure of Dennis Cooke. A North Carolina native, Messick came to Greenville from Montclair State Teachers College in New Jersey. He proved instrumental in East Carolina's growth during his tenure from 1947 to 1959, shepherding the school into a new era as East Carolina College. Messick's greatest contribution to Pirate football, hiring Leo Warren Jenkins—a talented administrator from Montclair State—would not be understood until several decades later.

The increased administrative responsibilities associated with athletic conference affiliation forced East Carolina to appoint a full-time athletics director in 1947. Messick selected Dr. Nephi M. Jorgensen (1909–1988) from California's Vallejo College for this endeavor. A health education professor and coach, Jorgensen directed Pirate athletics from 1947 to 1963, before transferring to the Department of Physical Education, where he remained until 1975. A devout Mormon, Jorgensen is credited with instilling a sense of moral and ethical responsibility amongst coaches and players. A Jorgensen family member worked at or attended East Carolina for 50 consecutive years, from 1947 to 1997. Dr. Jorgensen was inducted into the ECU Athletics Hall of Fame in 1974.

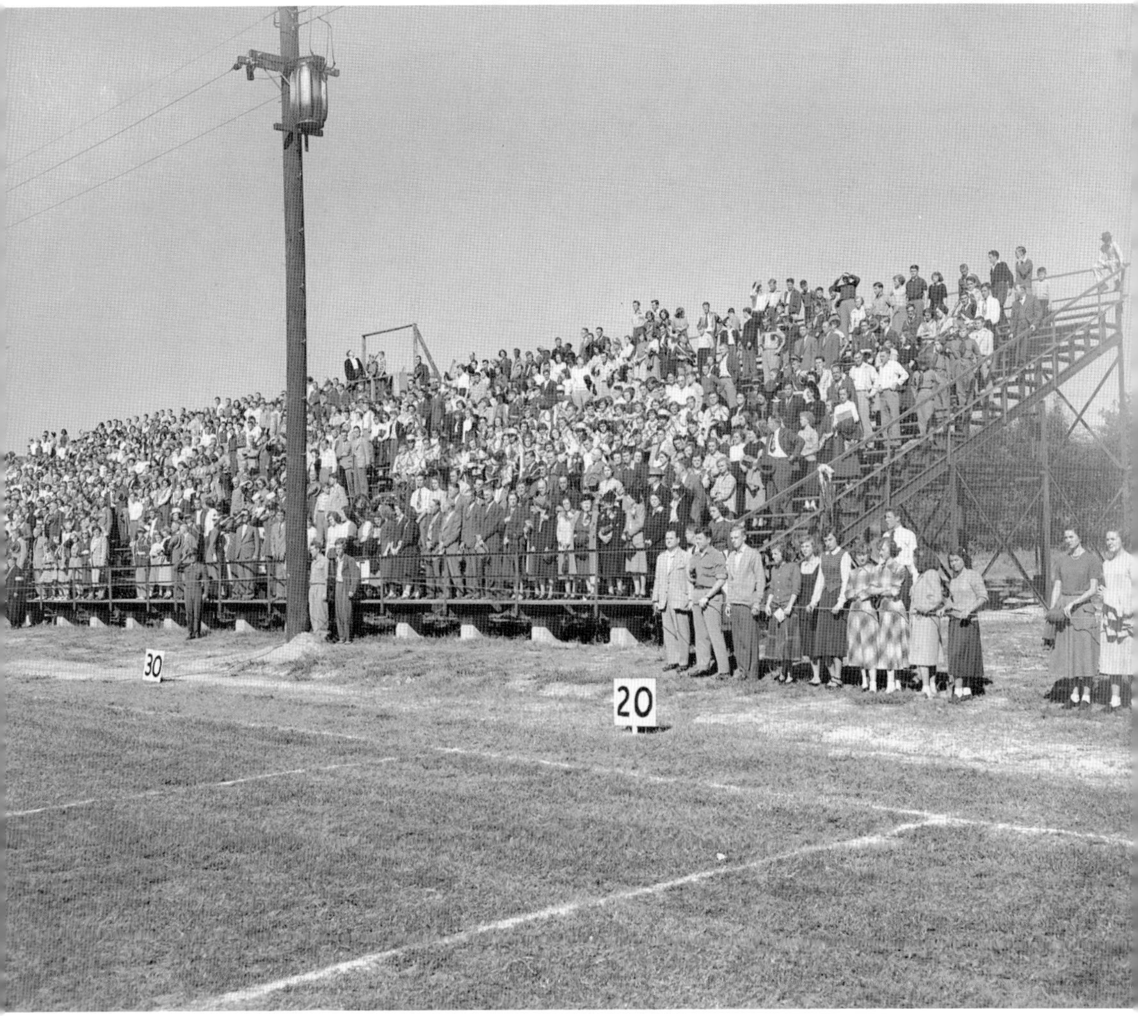

Prior to 1949, the Pirates played their home games at Guy Smith Stadium, a facility designed primarily for baseball, or on campus at Wright Field. Named for founding president Robert Wright, the field was reportedly 90 percent sand and 10 percent weeds. Acceptance into the North State Conference was met with requests that East Carolina construct a dedicated football stadium on campus. In November 1948, school officials and community leaders met on campus to discuss plans for a new $25,000 football stadium. The initial stadium construction meeting, led by local businessman and board of trustees member Edward E. Rawl, resulted in $8,000 in pledges. Within four months, 1,500 individuals and 227 businesses had surpassed the $25,000 goal. On September 21, 1949, College Stadium was formally dedicated on campus. On March 13, 1960, East Carolina dedicated the Rawl Building in honor of the former College Stadium chair Edward E. Rawl.

After Johnson's departure, Dr. Jorgensen selected William "Bill" Dole as the next Pirate football coach. Like Johnson, he served in the Navy and participated in the Iowa Pre-Flight school football program. Dole inherited a program that lost nine games the previous season. He cautioned the Pirate faithful to practice patience. The first game of the Dole era, which also happened to be the first game played in the new College Stadium, resulted in a 24-0 victory over the Marines of Cherry Point. Despite an overall losing record of 4-5-1 his first season, Dole demonstrated that the Pirates could compete under eligibility restrictions that came with membership in the North State Conference.

For their 1949 homecoming game, the Pirates welcomed Elon to Greenville. Despite the best efforts of All-Conference quarterback Roger Thrift, the Pirates fell 33-7, with their lone score coming off of a 14-yard pass from Thrift to halfback Jack Benzie.

An offensive innovator, Dole instituted a pass-first offense that excited Pirate fans and players alike. Here, several players cheer another East Carolina touchdown. Dole's aerial onslaught, at least by 1949 standards, saw the Pirates lead the North State Conference in pass attempts, completions, and touchdown passes.

Together, Bill Dole (right) and his assistant and eventual successor, Jack Boone (left), directed the Pirates to a 7-3 record in 1950. Football's growing popularity on campus is evident from the increased team coverage in both the campus newspaper and the yearbook. Students who rarely utilized the shuttle service to Guy Smith Stadium now regularly packed College Stadium, located on the southeast corner of campus.

Roger Thrift of Chapel Hill was the first prolific passer in Pirate history. He was selected by the Cleveland Browns with the 339th pick of the 1951 draft and thus became the first Pirate drafted into the National Football League. In 1977, he was inducted into the ECU Athletics Hall of Fame. His No. 36 is one of four jerseys retired by the Pirate football program.

The homecoming parade remains a major part of East Carolina homecoming festivities to this day. Here, two coeds proudly hoist a Jolly Roger as they ride a Pirate-themed car along the edge of campus on Fifth Street in 1951.

Unlike today's service academy teams, which follow NCAA eligibility rules, military teams of the 1950s were composed of a mix of former college and professional players as well as those new to the game. The quality of the teams varied from year to year, but their fighting spirit was always high. Here, Luke Taylor (No. 41, in white) assists in stopping a Cherry Point MCAS Flyer. The Pirate defense dominated this game, a 45-0 win for East Carolina. After a 4-6 season in 1951, Coach Dole resigned to accept the head coaching position at Davidson College.

The "Pirate Grid-Machine," as the 1953 yearbook referred to this squad, was the first postseason bowl team in school history. After finishing the year 6-2-2, they traveled to Salisbury, North Carolina, to compete in the first and only North Carolina Lion's Bowl against the undefeated Clarion State Teachers College Golden Eagles of Pennsylvania. The game reached halftime with a score of 6-6, with Sandy Siler scoring on a quarterback sneak, the only points the Pirates could muster in the first half. Clarion scored on the opening drive of the second half to make the score 13-6, which it remained until the final whistle. Despite the season-ending defeat, the Pirates returned to Greenville with renewed confidence.

Before the 1953 season, several media outlets favored the Pirates to win the North State Conference. Led by quarterback Dick Cherry (No. 32), the Pirates featured a talented backfield, including Paul Gay and Claude King. All three players are members of the ECU Athletics Hall of Fame.

Increased interest and rising attendance forced East Carolina to expand College Stadium by constructing two additional bleachers. Pictured here is a view from College Stadium with Christenbury Memorial Gymnasium in the background. Beyond the gymnasium is Tenth Street.

The Pirates' hard-hitting defense opened the 1953 season with shutouts of Wilson Teachers College and Lenoir-Rhyne. East Carolina followed their 45-25 homecoming victory with a dominant stretch in which their next three opponents' combined score reached a measly 14 points. Here, team leader Bobby Hodges tackles the Tampa Spartans' No. 70.

Having secured the North State Conference title, the Pirates headed to Florida to face the Tampa Spartans. Unfortunately, a last-minute Tampa interception ended Pirate hopes for an invitation to the Tangerine Bowl. A win over Stetson the following week inspired community leaders, along with Dr. Jorgensen, to organize the Greenville Elks Bowl. The game, which took place on January 2, 1954, resulted in a 12-0 defeat for the Pirates at the hands of the Morris Harvey Bears. Pictured here are the Elks Bowl team captains Bobby Hodges (No. 41) and Jack Britt (No. 22).

The Pirates began the 1954 season motivated to repeat as North State Conference champions, despite the loss of quarterback Dick Cherry to a season-ending injury in the preseason. In an effort to replace Cherry, Coach Boone rotated multiple players, including Boyd Webb (No. 24, right). Claude King and Emo Boado (No. 12, below) joined Webb in the backfield. Despite a rash of injuries, the Pirates faced Appalachian State on October 30 with the conference title at stake. The Mountaineers' 13-7 victory over the Pirates resulted in their taking the title. East Carolina played its final two games against teams from Florida to end the year.

Dick Cherry (No. 32) returned to lead the Pirates in the 1955 season. Playing behind an inexperienced offensive line, the "Blonde Bomber" could not repeat the success of the 1953 season. Coach Boone attempted to protect his QB by switching to a closed-T formation.

Despite a more conservative offense, split end Ray Pennington (in white) still managed to earn all-conference honors. In this feat, he was joined by Cherry and linebacker Lou Hallow. The Pirates finished the season 4-5 overall but 3-2 in conference play, with the two losses coming at the hands of Catawba and league winner Lenoir-Rhyne.

Senior linebacker Lou Hallow was the undisputed leader of the Pirate defense. At an intimidating 6 feet, 1 inch and 220 pounds, the Goldsboro native was reportedly the best linebacker Coach Boone ever met. Hallow displayed talent as both a defensive and offensive player, contributing to the offensive line as a starting center. After a career in Greenville that included recognition as a three-time Outstanding Defensive Player and as an All-North State Conference team selection, he was selected as the team's Most Valuable Player in 1955. That year, Hallow was also honored by the Associated Press as a first team Little All-American, the first All-American football player in East Carolina history. He was selected as the 306th pick of the 1955 NFL draft by the Los Angeles Rams. His NFL career never materialized, and after a stint in the US Marine Corps, Hallow returned to Greenville and was inducted into the ECU Athletics Hall of Fame in 1982.

The Pirates faced a season of difficult games in 1956. In an effort to increase exposure, Dr. Jorgensen added Virginia Tech and the University of Richmond to the schedule while phasing out military service teams. Despite schedule changes, certain rivalries continued. Pictured here, the Pirates' Gary Mattocks advances the football against the Western Carolina defense during the homecoming game. More than 12,000 fans packed College Stadium to witness the 20-19 victory over the Catamounts.

East Carolina defenders James Faircloth (No. 46) and Tommy Nash (No. 19) prepare to take on a Norfolk Navy ball carrier. The East Carolina helmets, featuring a hard plastic single-bar face mask, were modern by 1956 standards. In contrast, the Norfolk Navy helmets are the mask-less models that remained in use until the end of the decade.

The Pirates began their 1957 season with confidence. Hopes were diminished after consecutive season-opening losses to Richmond and to former coach Bill Dole's Davidson squad. Injuries in 1956 forced Boone to turn to underclassmen, providing them with valuable game experience, but the Davidson game proved to be the last for Dick Cherry as a Pirate. The standout quarterback was forced to withdraw from school to return home to aid his ailing parents. In this image, a referee spots the ball during the homecoming game against Elon as fullback Joe Holmes (No. 42) looks on. The Pirates lost their first homecoming game in six seasons in front of a crowd of 10,000 fans, marking their fourth straight loss of the year. The Pirates' lone victory that season was only secured in the final seconds of the season-ending game when Lee Atkinson hauled in a deep pass across the middle, racing to the end zone beyond the grasp of the Presbyterian defense.

Despite a dismal record, the Pirate faithful were treated to a magnificent season from halfback James Speight (No. 29, with ball). A Greenville native, Speight was responsible for nearly 75 percent of the Pirate touchdowns scored that season. He was inducted into the ECU Athletics Hall of Fame in 1981. His No. 29 is one of four retired numbers at East Carolina.

The Pirates remained in good spirits, as shown here. The Pirate youth movement continued, with the yearbook's sports editor referring to the 1957 squad as Jack Boone's "freshman-sophomore studded club."

Determined to put the one-win season behind them, Coach Boone and his Pirates spent countless hours practicing on College Stadium's field. Media outlets predicted future struggles for East Carolina, due in part to the graduation of the team's only all-conference selection, Ray Pennington.

Coach Boone and the Pirates prepare for their 1958 season finale against the Quakers of Guilford College on Thanksgiving Day. Guilford College, despite being in the same conference, refused to play East Carolina from 1954 to 1957. A raucous crowd in College Stadium witnessed a 20-0 victory, which culminated in a fireworks display. The win ended the Pirates' year with a record of 6-4.

Tackle Ed Emory (No. 48) and end Bill Cain (No. 35) co-captained the Pirates during the 1959 season. Emory, a dominant force along the line, started all four years he played at East Carolina. He was recognized as a third-team All-American his senior year. Emory returned to coach the Pirates from 1980 to 1984. Bill Cain earned recognition as an All-Carolina team selection in 1959. After graduation, Cain earned a master's degree from East Carolina before teaching and coaching at the high school level. He returned to campus in 1968 as head coach of the freshmen football team and served as the golf and tennis coach from 1972 to 1975. In 1975, Cain accepted the position of director of athletics, allowing him to oversee a stadium expansion and upgrade project. Both Emory and Cain are members of the ECU Athletics Hall of Fame.

The Pirates' recent successes, coupled with their veteran lineup, meant that the 1959 season would bring great enthusiasm for the team and its fans. This sign near the Christenbury driveway advertised the year's home games. The fire pit, which is behind the sign and slightly to the right, remains a prominent feature on campus, located just southeast of the Science and Technology Building along Tenth Street.

This image features a WNCT camera crew on scaffolding capturing the first televised game in College Stadium. Viewers tuned in to watch the 31-8 Pirate victory over Elon, and the emergence of televised home games contributed to the growing popularity of East Carolina football.

The Pirates opened the 1959 season with a loss to Presbyterian before embarking on a four-game winning streak with victories against Albright, Guilford College, Catawba, and Elon. Four straight defeats followed, ending hopes for a conference title. Here, James Speight (No. 29) tries to elude an Appalachian State defender.

Coach Boone could not mask his excitement when speaking to the media after a 74-0 win over Newport News Apprentice School. Fullback Mac Thacker (No. 33) looks on as his coach discusses the largest margin of victory in East Carolina history.

College president John Messick's sudden retirement in 1959 paved the way for the emergence of Leo Warren Jenkins (left) to become the fifth president of East Carolina College. A New Jersey native, Jenkins served in the US Marine Corps during World War II. During his service, he established an education program for soldiers serving in the Pacific theater. Jenkins was awarded the Bronze Star for his actions in combat during the Battle of Iwo Jima. While at East Carolina, Jenkins took an immediate interest in the athletics program, personally overseeing improvements in facilities, coaching staff, and equipment. A staunch football fan, Jenkins regularly led fans in cheers from the stands. One of his goals was to have East Carolina join the influential Southern Conference. His ambitions for East Carolina were not limited to athletics, however. He played a crucial role in obtaining university status, creating a world-class fine arts program, and establishing the Brody School of Medicine. In 1972, Leo Jenkins became the first chancellor of East Carolina University. In this 1961 image, Jenkins stands with Gov. Terry Sanford (right).

The Pirates opened the 1960 season with six consecutive victories despite losing standouts Ed Emory and James Speight. During the fifth game in that streak, Mac Thacker (No. 33) accounted for the homecoming game's only touchdown with a 90-yard interception return.

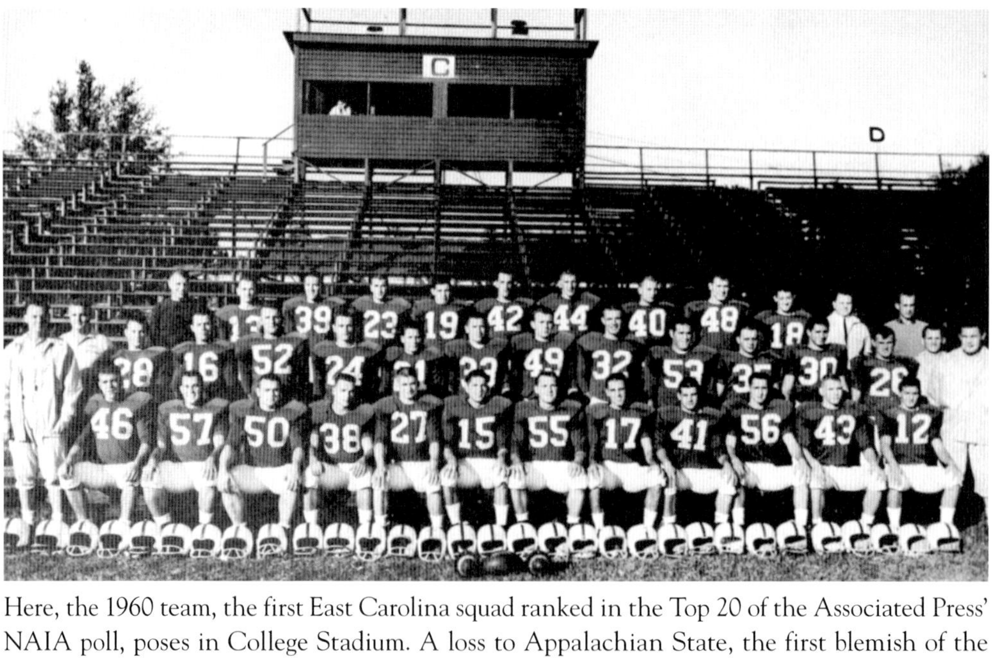

Here, the 1960 team, the first East Carolina squad ranked in the Top 20 of the Associated Press' NAIA poll, poses in College Stadium. A loss to Appalachian State, the first blemish of the season, dropped them from the rankings in late October. The Pirates finished the season with an overall record of 7-3.

In 1960, presidential candidate Sen. John F. Kennedy arrived on East Carolina's campus. Speaking to an assembled crowd in College Stadium on the morning of September 17, Kennedy drew cheers after mentioning that like East Carolina, he wanted to be a part of a "Southern Conference." Senators Sam Ervin and B. Everett Jordan, Gov. Luther Hodges, and gubernatorial candidate Terry Sanford joined Kennedy on stage for this campaign event. Leo Jenkins's role as Kennedy's campus host increased Jenkins's influence and raised East Carolina's profile, benefitting the future of athletics.

Halfback Larry Rudisill (No. 11) carries the ball against Elon in front of a packed College Stadium during the 1961 homecoming game. Rudisill scored on a 13-yard carry in the second half of the 22-20 win.

Coach Jack Boone is pictured here surrounded by his players during his final game, which ended in a tie with Wofford. The Pirates ended the 1961 season with a record of 5-4-1. Boone remained at East Carolina as an instructor in the Department of Physical Education, and in 1981 was inducted into the ECU Athletics Hall of Fame.

Tasked with replacing Coach Boone, Pres. Leo Jenkins turned to a familiar foe, Lenoir-Rhyne's Clarence Stasavich (at right above with an unidentified media member). A master of the single-wing offense, his Bear teams dominated the North State Conference, winning seven consecutive conference championships. The future coach starred on Lenoir-Rhyne's football and basketball teams during his college years. Born to Lithuanian immigrants, Stasavich served aboard a Landing Ship Tank with the US Navy during World War II and saw action in both theaters of the war.

The 1962 season marked the beginning of a new era for East Carolina football. First, the Pirates gained the coaching skills of Clarence Stasavich. Second, the success of Boone's squads and the growing student population led to a push for the construction of a new stadium. This image emphasizes the rapidly growing campus. The T-shaped structure at center is the Austin Building, which was constructed on the original football field. College Stadium, which was dedicated in 1949, is to the left. Rawl is the second T-shaped building at upper right. Also visible is Christenbury Memorial Gymnasium (upper left), Messick Theater Arts Building (right-hand side, near Austin and Rawl), and the frame of Speight Building next to the tennis courts.

Despite the best efforts of Bill Cline (No. 43) and his teammates, the opening game of the Stasavich era ended in a 27-26 win for the Spiders of Richmond. Also scoring for the Pirates were Larry Rudisill, Dave Bumgarner, and Jerry Tolley.

Jerry Tolley (No. 21) returns a punt against Western Carolina in Cullowhee. The Pirate loss put the team at 1-3 on the year. The Pirates would only play three home dates that season, owing to their withdrawal from the Carolinas Conference, previously known as the North State Conference. Tolley went on to coach at Elon following his playing days, winning national championships in 1980 and 1981.

This photograph, taken from the stands during the last game played in College Stadium, memorializes a 29-12 win over the Eastern Kentucky Maroons. The victory ensured Stasavich a winning campaign, as the team rallied to finish 5-4 on the year. The most disappointing loss of that year (7-6) came from Coach Stasavich's former team, Lenoir-Rhyne. A missed extra point accounted for the margin of defeat. With a year of the complicated single-wing offense under their belts and a new stadium on the way, the Pirates closed the 1962 season on a high note.

3

FIND ME IN FICKLEN

On September 21, 1963, Dr. Leo Jenkins formally dedicated the newly constructed James S. Ficklen Memorial Stadium. In attendance were many of the Pirates who made the event possible, including former coaches Jack Boone, Jim Johnson, and Ken Beatty. With seating for 10,000, Ficklen Stadium nearly tripled the capacity of old College Stadium. In this image, Coach Stasavich is handed the keys to a new Chevrolet Impala, the first complimentary car given to any East Carolina coach.

The ground-breaking ceremony for James S. Ficklen Stadium occurred on May 3, 1962. Lucy Warren Myers Ficklen turned the first dirt pile using the same shovel reportedly used by Gov. Thomas Jordan Jarvis at East Carolina's ground-breaking ceremony in 1908. Pictured here with Ficklen are, from left to right, (first row) Wally Howard, unidentified, Leo Jenkins, Herbert Waldrop, Ficklen, James S. Ficklen Jr., and W.H. Scales; (second row) Dave Whichard, two unidentified, Reynolds May, unidentified, Fitzhugh Duncan, and unidentified.

From left to right, John "Jack" Minges, Dr. Leo Jenkins, and W.H. "Booger" Scales celebrate in New York City's Copacabana Lounge in October 1963. Minges and Scales led the community stadium drive that raised over $280,000 for the construction of Ficklen Stadium, exceeding the established goal of $200,000.

Students and members of the community also supported the stadium drive. Here, two ladies collect spent cigarette packs from campus. The Liggett & Myers tobacco company donated 1¢ for each empty pack.

James Skinner Ficklen (1900–1955) was the son of E.B. Ficklen, founder of the Greenville tobacco company by the same name. Ficklen worked for his father's company in addition to serving on the board of trustees for the consolidated University of North Carolina for 14 years. Ficklen also served on the board of directors for Guarantee Bank (later Wachovia Bank) and the Greenville Home Building and Loan Association. He was a member of the Greenville Water and Light Commission and a founder of the Greenville Country Club.

The south side of Ficklen Stadium featured a press box and modern stadium seating that could accommodate 10,000 fans. The bleachers from College Stadium were moved to the north side of Ficklen Stadium to seat visiting crowds. The total cost of the stadium was $283,387.

Leo Jenkins (left) and Clarence Stasavich (right) proudly display a rendering of an enlarged Ficklen Stadium. The original stadium, designed by the Greenville architectural firm of Dudley & Shoe, featured 58 rows of seats.

Two ladies sell tickets to the first game at Ficklen Stadium near Brody's Department Store in downtown Greenville. Proceeds from these tickets went to support the local Methodist Boy's Home.

The Pirates faced Wake Forest after a season-opening loss to Richmond in Virginia. The Deacons' visit to Greenville marked the first by an Atlantic Coast Conference team. Here, fullback Tom Michel outruns the Deacon defense to score one of his three touchdowns of the game.

Facing Western Carolina before a crowd of over 11,000, the Pirates entered the 1963 homecoming game with a record of 4-1. Stasavich's single-wing offense was on full display as the Pirates scored 36 points in the first half before going on to win the game 50-0.

Clarence Stasavich (left) and Nephi Jorgensen discuss the 1963 football season in Dr. Jorgensen's office. Although Stasavich replaced Jorgensen as athletic director, the latter was still a member of the athletic department administration. With a new stadium and an impressive winning streak, Greenville was bursting with Pirate pride. Stores and homes often displayed their loyalty in the form of season ticket holder stickers, the precursor to the Pirate Club decals that remain a symbol of school spirit today.

Maurice Allen (No. 48) shares the play call as the Pirates huddle against Lenoir-Rhyne. Stasavich emerged victorious in his second try against his old team, this time using a new formation that featured a split end. The tactical move paid off as Buddy Bodander scored on a 33-yard pass.

In the final game of the regular season, the Pirates traveled to Tampa riding an eight game winning streak. Here, Dinky Mills (No. 24) carries the ball against the stout Spartan defense. The defensive battle ended with the Pirates winning 14-8, thus securing a birth in the Eastern Bowl.

The Pirates traveled to Allentown, Pennsylvania, to play against Boston's Northeastern Huskies in the Eastern Bowl (known as the Cement Bowl until 1963). Bowl organizers selected the Pirates to face the 1963 ECAC champions partially as a result of Stasavich's reputation and popularity. The Huskies entered the game with a perfect 8-0 record. A winter storm in the week preceding the game froze the field, and fans shivered in the bitter cold. Johnny Anderson (No. 84) set up the first Pirate touchdown after his eight-yard carry put the ball at the Huskies' 15 yard line. Perhaps finally accustomed to the arctic conditions, East Carolina scored three straight touchdowns, including two on runs of more than 80 yards to complete the scoring. When the final whistle sounded, the Pirates had secured their first bowl victory with a final score of 27-6. Tom Michel, in his final game at East Carolina, was named the game's MVP. Michel was drafted by the Minnesota Vikings the following spring.

Clarence Stasavich (far left) and Leo Jenkins (third from left) discuss matters with unidentified men during the Southern Conference annual meeting in May 1964. East Carolina's application for admission was accepted, with the 1964 season serving as a probationary period. Though many of the premier large programs left to form the Southeastern (SEC) and Atlantic Coast (ACC) Conferences, the Southern Conference still boasted well-regarded programs, including George Washington, Richmond, William and Mary, the Citadel, Davidson, Furman, and West Virginia. That summer, Stasavich pushed his team through grueling two-a-day practices under the scorching eastern North Carolina sun to prepare them for the upcoming season. The excitement on campus was noticeable, with one yearbook writer calling attention to the "prestige and status" that accompanied the new conference affiliation.

The 1964 team poses on the steps of Christenbury Memorial Gymnasium. They carried an undefeated record through most of October, before suffering a 22-20 loss to Richmond, snapping a 14-game winning streak.

Bill Cline (No. 43) looks downfield to an open Dave Bumgarner (No. 87) as the Pirates face the Citadel Bulldogs in Charleston, South Carolina, on Halloween. The Pirates followed their victory with consecutive wins over Furman and Presbyterian at home, ending the regular season at 8-1.

In 1964, the Pirates accepted an invitation to participate in the Tangerine Bowl in Orlando, Florida. A large crowd cheered on their beloved Pirates, some proudly displaying handmade banners, as the team prepared to board a plane headed for the game.

Students and supporters traveled by train to Orlando to support the Pirates and enjoy some warm Florida weather.

Team captains meet for the pregame coin toss. East Carolina, in white, received the game's opening kickoff. Representing the Pirates are split end Dave Bumgarner (No. 87) and offensive tackle Ted Day (No. 74).

The referee signals an East Carolina touchdown as Bill Cline reaches the end zone in the fourth quarter, putting the Pirates down 13-12. They then took the lead on a successful two-point conversion with Cline finding an open Pete Crane with a pass to conclude the day's scoring and win the game.

Dave Bumgarner (left) and Bill Cline celebrate following their victory in the Tangerine Bowl. Cline earned the MVP award along with recognition as an AP Little All-American. Ted Day and Dave Bumgarner were recognized by the AP as Honorable Mentions. Upon their return to Greenville, the triumphant Pirates were greeted by 1,200 fans at the Greenville Airport. A human corridor formed, and each Pirate was greeted with banners and handshakes as they made their way to the buses that would carry them back to campus. As a testament to his winning strategy, Stasavich moved through the welcoming crowd wearing a button that simply read, "We Try Harder."

In 1964, Stasavich (far right) received the highest honor bestowed on football coaches: Kodak's NCAA College Division Coach of the Year Award. His three-season record at East Carolina (24-6), capped by consecutive bowl victories, earned him the distinction. With him are, from left to right, Kodak vice president Gerald B. Zornow, coach Ara Parseghian of the University of Notre Dame, and coach Frank Broyles of the University of Arkansas. It was the first year voting ended in a tie for the university division since the award's establishment in 1935. Parseghian retired as Notre Dame's coach in 1974 with 170 career victories. He was inducted into the College Football Hall of Fame in 1980. Broyles coached at Arkansas from 1958 to 1976 and served as athletic director from 1974 to 2007. He was inducted into the College Football Hall of Fame in 1983.

Few visitors to Greenville in 1965 could fail to notice the school spirit prevalent throughout town. Among the most memorable sights for students and residents was the Stadium Cleaners Laundromat sign along Tenth Street.

The 1965 season marked East Carolina's official entry into the Southern Conference. The Pirates opened conference play with a loss to Furman, despite the efforts of this unidentified ball carrier.

Ever the perfectionist, Stasavich shares strategy with his offensive line during a time out against the Citadel. A 21-0 score earned the Pirate defense their first shutout of the season, pushing their regular season record to 4-1. Four consecutive wins followed, setting up a return to the Tangerine Bowl.

The key to the 1965 Pirate offense was bruising senior fullback Dave Alexander (No. 31, with ball). The Washington, DC, native ran for 1,029 yards on the season, thus becoming the first Pirate to surpass the 1,000-yard benchmark. He was inducted into the ECU Athletics Hall of Fame in 1975.

The defending Tangerine Bowl champions returned to Orlando to face the University of Maine Black Bears. Representing the Pirates for the coin toss were Norman Swindell (No. 18) and Mitchell Cannon (No. 69). The Pirates led 10-0 at the half, with a field goal and touchdown reception, both from 35 yards out.

Norman Swindell clears a path for Dave Alexander against the Maine defense. Alexander accounted for three second-half touchdowns, two rushing and one pass, finishing the game with 206 yards of total offense. His performance in this, his final game for East Carolina, earned him the game MVP honors. The final score: East Carolina 31, Maine 0, securing consecutive Tangerine Bowl titles for the Pirates.

The Pirates had little time to revel in three consecutive 9-1 seasons, each capped by a bowl victory, before tragedy befell the team. During the winter break, senior Norman Swindell was killed in a duck hunting mishap near Lukens Island, along the South River in North Carolina. A massive Coast Guard surface and air search recovered his skiff along with the body of his hunting companion John Foxx. Swindell, a team captain, was 21 years old at the time and had been recognized with the Southern Conference's Jacobs trophy, given to the best blocker in the league.

Despite the loss of many standout players from the Tangerine Bowl teams, expectations for the 1966 season were high. To prepare his team for the rigors of the season, Stasavich ran very physical practices, as evident from this photograph of a preseason blocking drill.

The Pirates return to the huddle during a muddy game against Richmond. Despite earning a share of the Southern Conference title with a record of 4-1-1, the Pirates lost every non-conference game to finish the season 4-5-1. It was Stasavich's first losing season in 12 years.

The Pirates entered the 1967 season in good spirits. Leading the cheers that season was 1967 Miss Cheerleader USA Sherry Robertson, posing here with a smiling Coach Stasavich before a game.

Tailback Neal Hughes (No. 43) proved to be a stellar athlete, playing both football and baseball for the Pirates. Here, he evades Wildcat defenders in front of a record-setting crowd at Davidson.

The Citadel Bulldogs (dark tops) spoiled the Pirates' (white tops) homecoming game, halting East Carolina's six-game winning streak before an estimated 17,000 fans. The loss ended the Pirates' chance of an undefeated season. The Pirates rebounded the following week, defeating Furman at home with a powerful 292-yard rushing attack. Next, the West Texas A&M Buffaloes' speedy running back Eugene "Mercury" Morris led his team to a 37-13 win over East Carolina in Greenville. With no potential bowl games, the Pirates closed out the season on the road against winless Marshall in West Virginia. Willard "Butch" Colson of Elizabeth City, North Carolina, ran 117 yards for the Pirates, setting a single-season Southern Conference record with 1,135 yards total. Colson finished his career in Greenville with 2,512 rushing yards after the 1969 season. The Pirates finished the year 8-2 overall and 4-1 in conference, placing them in second behind West Virginia. Colson was inducted into the ECU Athletics Hall of Fame in 1998.

Co-captains W. Lineberry and Bennett Grieb, along with Parsons College players, watch the opening coin flip of the 1968 season. The season started off on a high note, but injuries contributed to four straight losses, ending any bowl hopes by mid-season.

Players confer on the sidelines during a game against Louisiana Tech. Facing future NFL Hall of Fame quarterback Terry Bradshaw, the Pirates played 10 first-time starters. The lineup changes fell short, however, and the Pirates lost the game 35-7.

During the homecoming game against Tampa, Billy Wightman (No. 45) holds his gaze downfield as Butch Colson (No. 34) keeps his path clear. The game was a tale of two halves, with the Pirates leading 21-0 at halftime but finding themselves down 28-21 at the sound of the final whistle.

George Whitley (No. 20) runs through the Marshall defense with this carry. A previously stagnant Pirate offense exploded for 49 points to win over the Thundering Herd. A win against the Citadel was followed by a loss to East Tennessee, leaving the Pirates with a losing record of 4-6.

Fans expected a return to glory in 1969 as media outlets speculated about a possible conference title and Tangerine Bowl appearance. Despite high hopes and the best efforts of Leyton Getsinger and Brandy the Poodle, Pirate fans found few opportunities to celebrate. A season-opening loss to East Tennessee began a four-game streak that was eventually broken by consecutive wins over Furman and Davidson. Another three-game losing streak brought the East Carolina record to 2-7 as the year ended. Stasavich's vaunted single wing averaged only 12 points per contest with the defense surrendering more than 28 points per game on the season. Still, several Pirates managed to distinguish themselves with individual performances. Defensive tackle George Wheeler was recognized as All-Southern Conference. Butch Colson gained 1,003 yards from scrimmage on the year and finished his career with two conference records and seven school records.

After experiencing consecutive losing seasons for the first time since his arrival in Greenville, Stasavich was forced to recognize the difficulties of simultaneously serving as head football coach and athletic director. A victim of his own success, Stasavich recognized the necessity of hiring a full-time athletics director. He resigned from his post as football coach two days after the season ended. Stasavich finished with a total 170 career wins, which trailed only Bear Bryant and John Vaught.

From left to right are Clarence Stasavich, Mike McGee, and Leo Jenkins announcing McGee as the new head football coach on December 19, 1969. A former All-American lineman and Outland Trophy winner at Duke, McGee played for the St. Louis Cardinals in the NFL from 1960 to 1962.

Rusty Scales (No. 24) carries the ball in front of 28,350 fans in East Carolina's first ever meeting with the NC State Wolfpack. That highly anticipated contest bred a rivalry that, despite irregular meetings, has lasted more than four decades.

Billy Wallace (No. 33) carries the ball in the homecoming game against Southern Illinois. The Salukis spoiled East Carolina's homecoming and prevented McGee from earning his first coaching win. The Pirates finished the season 3-8. McGee resigned after the season to accept the head coaching job at Duke, his alma mater.

After McGee's resignation, his former assistant, Ulmo "Sonny" Randle, took over as the Pirates' head coach. Randle played wide receiver at the University of Virginia and enjoyed a 10-year NFL career as a member of the Cardinals organization, highlighted by four selections to the Pro Bowl from 1960 to 1962 and again in 1965.

Randle stalks the sidelines during a William and Mary game. Randle instituted a triple option using a split backfield. Enduring growing pains with a new coach and system, the Pirates started the season with three losses before a thrilling comeback victory over the Citadel righted the ship.

The Pirates carry a victorious Coach Randle off the field after a 31-15 win over NC State in Raleigh. It was East Carolina's first win over the in-state rival and endeared Randle to Pirate fans who had endured multiple losing streaks against in-state opponents in the years prior.

The 1971 Pirates' offensive backfield watches their defensive teammates during a game against Furman. Consisting of, from left to right, Les Strayhorn, Rusty Scales, Carlester Crumpler, and Billy Wallace, the Pirate offensive backfield skillfully ran Randle's triple option to rack up yards and points.

An ABC network camera crew takes advantage of a vehicle strategically parked behind the Pirate bench to film a game against the Citadel. The Pirates finished 4-6 the previous year, but signs pointed to a program on the rise. New offensive coordinator Viggo Ragazzo instituted the I formation to better take advantage of the running of Carlester Crumpler and Les Strayhorn. Future NFL quarterback Carl Summerell ensured that the aerial component of the East Carolina offense was equally effective. Defensive assistant coach John Matlock christened the defensive group the "Wild Dogs." Led by middle linebacker Danny Kepley, the unit earned a reputation for attacking the football with abandon. The undersized unit finished the season as the nation's leader in total defense and rushing defense. Kepley went on to star in the Canadian Football League (CFL) with the Edmonton Eskimos. He was inducted into the CFL Hall of Fame in 1996.

Two unidentified Pirates hoist the trophy awarded to the Southern Conference champions. A perfect 6-0 mark in conference play contributed to a successful 7-2 campaign, with both losses coming to in-state opponents, UNC and NC State.

Carlester Crumpler (No. 32) carries the ball in the 1973 season opener against NC State in front of 40,500 fans, the largest crowd at NC State's Carter Stadium to that date. NC State won in a rout. Coach Randle claimed responsibility for the stinging defeat. The Pirates shook off the loss and won their next six games.

Wild Dogs Danny Kepley (No. 42) and Mike Cruisie (No. 48) converge on a Tar Heel ball carrier. A back-and-forth game ended when Pirate kicker Jim Woody's 53-yard attempt fell short as time expired, giving UNC a one-point victory. Despite the loss, the Pirates earned the respect of their ACC foe.

Coach Randle ponders his next move while being shadowed by offensive lineman Dan Killebrew (No. 70). The coach repeated his feat of the previous year, winning the Southern Conference title. He resigned days after the season ended to accept the head coaching position at his alma mater, the University of Virginia.

Seen here is Pat Dye (center) being introduced as the Pirates' next football coach. Also shown are Chancellor Leo Jenkins (left), chairman of the ECU board of trustees Roddy Jones (right), and members of the football team (standing). ECU was Dye's first head coaching position. He had previously served as a defensive assistant at the University of Alabama under the legendary Paul "Bear" Bryant.

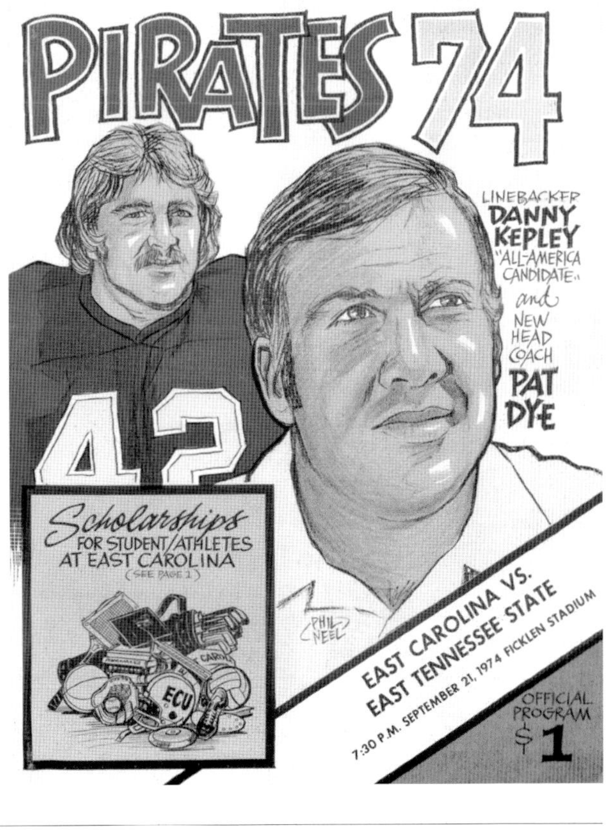

Dye's hiring excited both the program staff and the Pirate fan base. A rising star in the collegiate coaching ranks, Dye's popularity was enhanced even more by his appearance with fan favorite Danny Kepley on this game-day program cover.

Quarterback Mike Weaver (No. 9) eludes a sack by the Citadel defense. Dye brought the wishbone formation to Greenville from Tuscaloosa. The option offense used misdirection to neutralize larger, more athletic defenses.

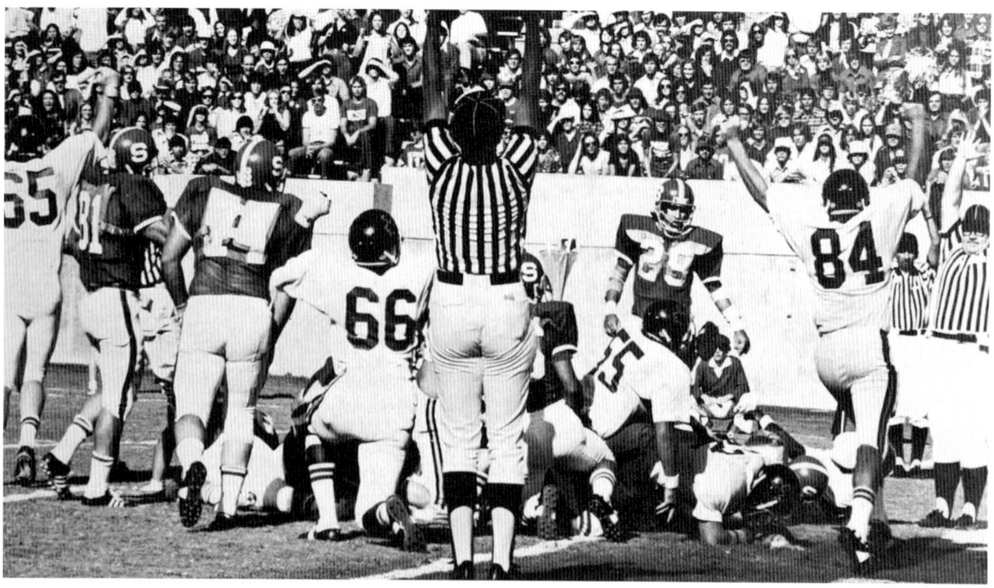

Touchdown, East Carolina! The Pirates cross the goal line against NC State, albeit in a losing effort. They finished the year 3-3 in conference play and 7-4 overall. More importantly, they began the off-season with Pat Dye, one of the preeminent recruiters of the day.

Willie Bryant (No. 75) and Cary Godette (No. 76) converge on a Western Carolina ball carrier during the 1975 homecoming game, winning a 42-14 Pirate victory. The triumph pushed ECU to 4-3, setting the stage for a strong finish to the season.

Defensive end Zach Valentine (No. 89) sets the edge as Furman's quarterback goes down for a sack by an unidentified East Carolina defender. Dye praised his team's defensive effort, commenting that they had "come of age" in the second half of the season.

Eddie Hicks (No. 28) carries the ball around the right end against UNC during this 53-yard touchdown run. The Pirates traveled to Chapel Hill with heavy hearts in 1975. The day before their game against the Tar Heels, athletic director and former coach Clarence Stasavich passed away from complications following a heart attack. Although many fans suggested a game cancellation, Helen Stasavich convinced Chancellor Leo Jenkins that the team should play in honor of her late husband, urging the Pirates to "just win it." Thousands made the journey to Chapel Hill to cheer on the Pirates and honor their former coach. A Tar Heel touchdown on the game's first possession was answered by three consecutive East Carolina first-quarter scores. A 21-17 halftime lead stretched to 38-17 by the game's end. A jubilant Coach Dye distributed victory cigars that he had secretly packed for the trip, as Chancellor Jenkins cheered with the visiting Pirate fans. After the game, Dye paid his respects to Stasavich on the field. The eastbound convoy carrying the Pirates to Greenville celebrated the program's first victory over UNC during their 120-mile trip home. East Carolina won its three remaining games, including a 61-10 upset over Randle's Virginia squad, to finish the season 8-3.

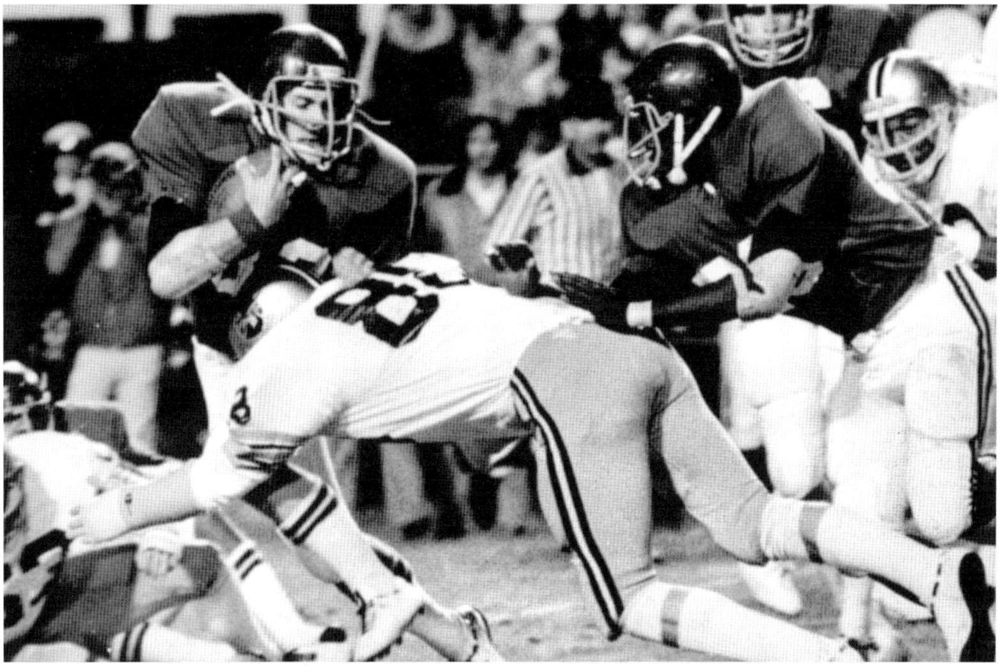

Vince Kolanko (No. 32) advances against the Appalachian State defense, helping earn a victory in the final game of the 1976 season. The Pirates finished the year with an overall record of 9-2.

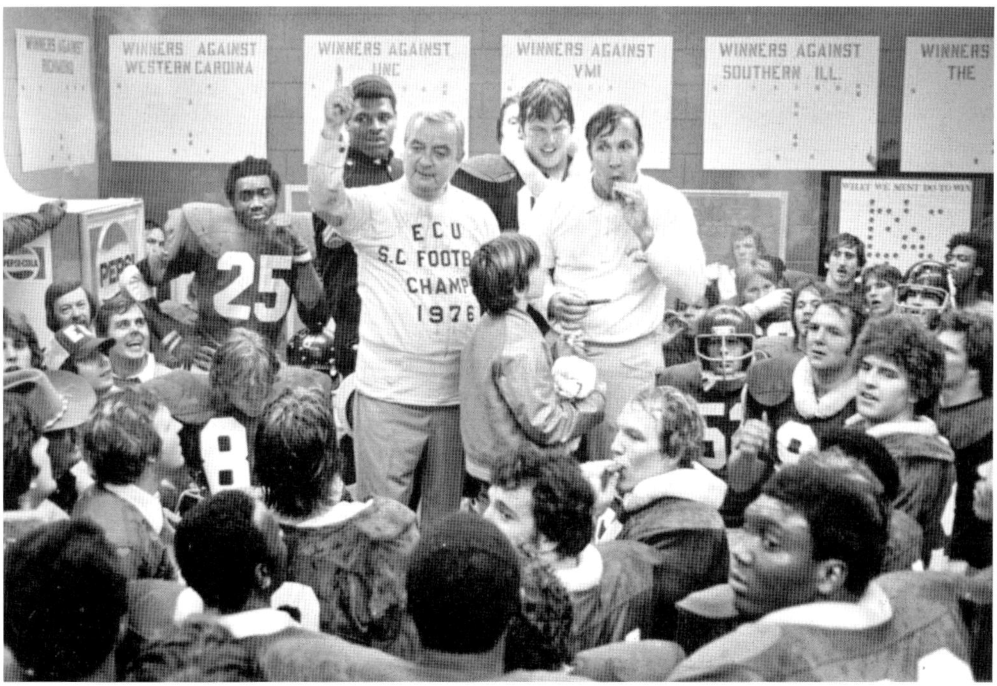

A 6-1 record in conference play earned the Pirates their final Southern Conference title as Leo Jenkins (gesturing) and Pat Dye (with cigar) celebrate with the team in the locker room. The Pirates left the Southern Conference in 1977 after the NCAA reconfigured its classification system.

Leander Green follows his blockers despite having his jersey ripped off by the Marshall defense in a failed attempt to take him down. The Pirates won handily, 45-0, bringing their season record to 8-3 and earning an invitation to the Independence Bowl.

Defensive linemen John Morris (No. 83), Rocky Butler (No. 98), and Mindell Tyson (No. 94) show off their custom bowl game jerseys. The Pirates faced the Louisiana Tech Bulldogs in Shreveport, Louisiana. The Independence Bowl game marked the first for East Carolina since the 1965 Tangerine Bowl.

A bowl game official watches over the coveted Independence Bowl trophy, as 18,200 fans packed State Fair Stadium. In the second meeting between ECU and Louisiana Tech, the Pirates took an early lead with touchdown runs of three yards, one yard, and one yard to take a 21-0 lead in the second quarter. The Bulldogs answered with consecutive scores, sending the teams to their locker rooms at halftime with a score of 21-10. A third quarter Tech field goal ended the Bulldogs' scoring as Pirate fullback Theodore Sutton rumbled 45 yards into the end zone, followed by a three-yard scoring run by quarterback Leander Green. The Pirates took home the trophy with a final score of 35-13. Sutton finished with a touchdown and 17 carries for an Independence Bowl record of 143 yards, earning him MVP status. Green and Anthony Collins each reached the end zone twice. On defense, Zach Valentine was named outstanding player for leading the team with seven tackles. The Pirates held the Bulldogs to only 275 yards of total offense and forced seven turnovers.

As East Carolina's program grew, so did the accompanying pageantry surrounding the team. Here, Janet Swain, Lynn Williford, and Cathy Dreyer entertain the crowd during halftime as the marching band plays in the background.

Former chancellor Leo Jenkins (left) and ECU's new chancellor Thomas Brewer (right) appear at the ground-breaking ceremony for ECU's Brody School of Medicine. Brewer replaced Jenkins as chancellor following Jenkins's mandatory resignation in 1978. While he professed his support for athletics, Brewer clashed with Coach Dye over the importance of the football program to East Carolina. Dye resigned as coach in 1979.

4

The Modern Era

Ed Emory leads the Pirates onto the field. The former Pirate standout was chosen to replace Dye as ECU's head coach. Emory recruited a bevy of talented young assistants, including future Clemson coach Tommy Bowden. Emory's choice for special teams coordinator especially excited Pirate fans. For this role, he hired his former coach, Jack Boone, who had been teaching in the physical education department. Boone's new position made him the most senior member of Emory's coaching staff.

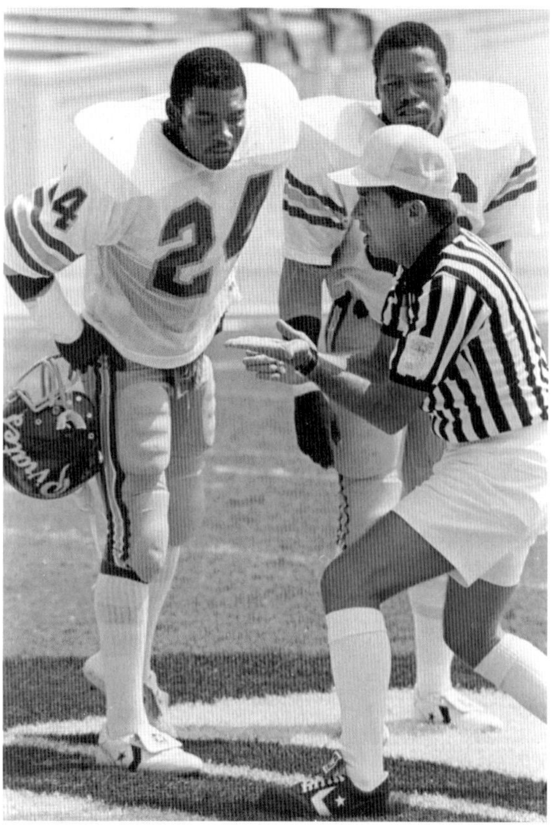

Emory earned a reputation as a hardworking and tough player, particularly after recovering from a career-threatening injury. His efforts to improve practice habits included establishing a dedicated weight room and hiring a strength coach. The Pirates finished 4-7 in his first season at the helm.

East Carolina's team captains await the coin toss at Duke's Wallace Wade Stadium in 1981. The Blue Devils won that day, evening the head-to-head record between the schools at 2-2. Duke and ECU first played in 1977.

Quarterback Calton Nelson (No. 8) evades the Southwestern Louisiana defense in Lafayette. The Pirates won 35-31. In his second year as coach, Emory improved by one win, finishing the year 5-6.

A nontraditional float makes its way down Fifth Street during the 1982 homecoming parade. The converted golf cart led a convoy of trucks, convertibles, and towed trailers along the edge of campus, exciting Pirate fans for their homecoming game against Illinois State.

Determined to avoid a third straight losing campaign, Emory vowed to evaluate the program from top to bottom. He discarded the wishbone offense and implemented a freeze option offense. This development traded the third running back for an additional wide receiver, opening more passing options. The changes successfully rejuvenated the Pirate offense, which had stagnated the previous few seasons.

Quarterback Greg Stewart (No. 15) holds as kicker Jeff Heath attempts a field goal against William and Mary during the 1982 season. The Pirates were undefeated at home that season, finishing the year 7-4. Two of the losses were to AP-ranked opponents, No. 19 Florida State and No. 18 West Virginia.

East Carolina's mascot PeeDee the Pirate poses in Ficklen Stadium. PeeDee first appeared in 1983 and was named following a contest involving Pitt County schoolchildren. The moniker was inspired by two rivers that flow through the Carolinas bearing that name. In response to ECU student complaints concerning their lack of involvement in the name selection process, the name "PeeDee" was officially dropped in 1985, and the mascot became known simply as "The Pirate." Nevertheless, the name PeeDee is still commonly used when referring to the character. In 2008, PeeDee received a minor makeover, appearing fitter and brighter for his 25th season roaming the sidelines and stands.

In 1983, standout offensive lineman Terry Long was East Carolina's first AP First Team All-American. The former paratrooper was drafted by the Pittsburgh Steelers in 1984; he played for eight seasons.

The Pirates stop a Gator threat during a game in Gainesville, Florida. Emory's innovative trap offense powered the Pirates to one of the most successful seasons in team history. An 8-3 record, with all three losses being narrow ones against AP Top 10 teams, led to ECU's No. 20 ranking in the final poll of the year.

Tyrone Johnson (No. 47) drags down a Georgia Southern running back in a 1984 game. The Pirates earned their first win of the season, 34-27, after a 0-3 start. Despite a miracle season the previous year, the Pirate fan base soon turned on Emory as the losses increased.

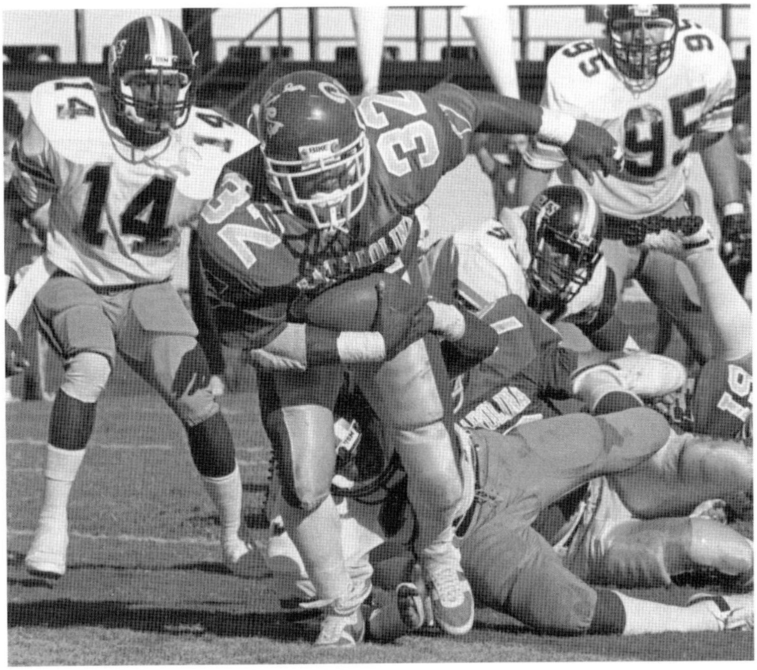

Reggie Branch (No. 32) darts across the goal line in the final game of the 1984 season against Southern Mississippi. This game marked Emory's last as a Pirate coach. He was released after a 2-9 season and would never again coach in the college ranks.

Art Baker was hired as the next coach of the ECU Pirates. Baker served as Emory's offensive coordinator in 1983 and held the same position at Florida State in 1984. He had also served as the head coach at Furman and the Citadel.

Seen here is the view from the SW Texas State defense as they face the Pirates. The Baker era opened with consecutive wins against NC State and SW Texas State. The following week, a close loss to No. 10 Penn State began a nine-game slide to end the year, once again, at 2-9.

With Ficklen Stadium in the background, cheerleaders lead a pirate ship through the tailgating lot before the 1986 homecoming game. Baker's Pirates finished the year 2-9 for the third consecutive year.

ECU fans celebrate on the goal posts in Carter-Finley Stadium after upsetting the Wolfpack in 1987. NC State athletic director Jim Valvano suspended the series following the incident. The teams would not face each other again until the 1992 Peach Bowl.

Cheerleaders and football players run onto the Ficklen Stadium field with the victory bell before a 1988 contest. Minges Coliseum is visible in the background. After a 3-8 season, Baker's contract was not renewed. Despite being well liked, Baker's 12-32 record in Greenville required that the Pirates chart a new course.

University of Georgia defensive coordinator Bill Lewis was introduced as the 16th head football coach at East Carolina on December 3, 1988. He boasted one previous stint as a head coach, with the University of Wyoming from 1977 to 1979, before joining Vince Dooley's staff in Athens.

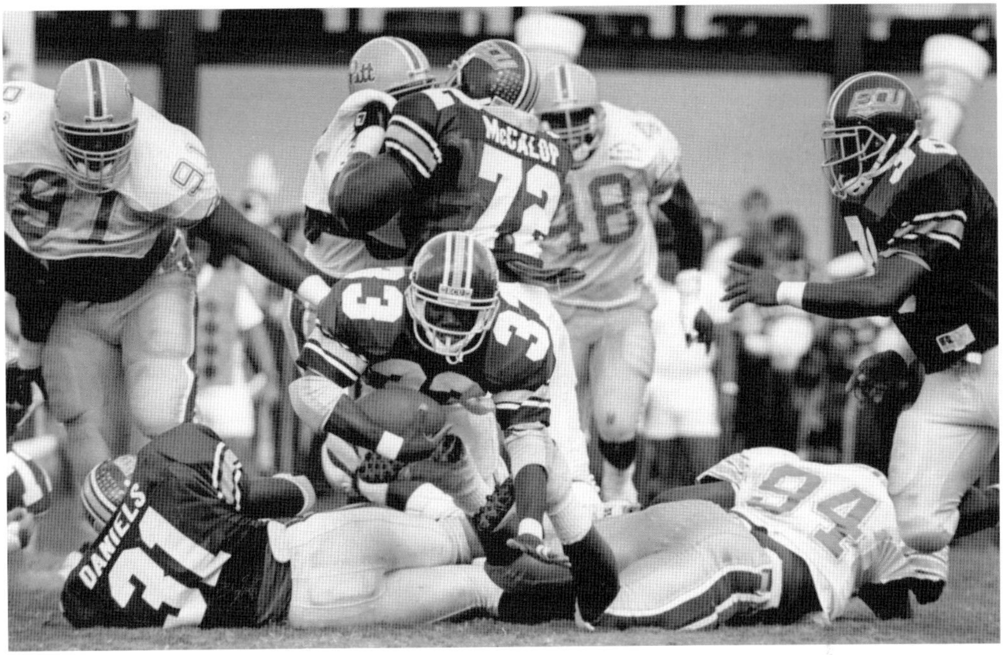

The Pirates attack the Pittsburgh defense with a rushing attempt in a 1989 game. East Carolina began the year with three wins before settling for a tie with Louisiana Tech. They finished the year 5-5-1, their first non-losing season since 1983.

Pictured is a view inside a team huddle before a 1990 contest against a Southern Mississippi team quarterbacked by Brett Favre. The Pirates finished the year 5-6, with near upsets of Virginia Tech and Georgia hinting at the magical season that would follow.

Jeff Blake (No. 2) prepares to launch a pass deep downfield. A widely recruited high school athlete, the Florida native chose to attend East Carolina over offers from Florida and Florida State so that he could play as a quarterback. The rocket-armed passer started a single game in 1988, as a slot back. He played in seven games in 1989, with one start against Miami. He entered the 1990 season as the full-time starter and showed flashes of promise as the team endured a 2-5 start. In the homecoming game versus Cincinnati, Blake threw for 199 yards and ran for 119 more. The dual-threat quarterback's coming out party would continue through the remainder of the 1990 season. In 1991, Blake emerged as a bona fide star, throwing for a then school record 3,073 yards. He was also recognized as a second-team All-American and finished ninth in the Heisman Trophy voting. Inducted into the ECU Athletics Hall of Fame in 2007, Blake enjoyed a 14-year NFL career highlighted by selection for the 1996 Pro Bowl.

Pirate players and coach Bill Lewis hold aloft the trophy presented to the winners of the 1992 Peach Bowl. The 1991 season opened with an ESPN televised loss to the University of Illinois. A five-game winning streak that included an upset over No. 15 Syracuse in the Carrier Dome had the Pirates ranked No. 20 for the first time since the 1983 season. The winning streak continued for another five games as the Pirates steadily climbed higher in the AP poll. They finished the regular season at 10-1 and ranked No. 12 in the nation. Playing on New Year's Day, the Wolfpack held a 34-17 lead two minutes into the final quarter. A Blake touchdown run was followed by a touchdown pass to Dion Johnson. After holding the Pack offense, ECU scored on another touchdown pass with tight end Luke Fisher dragging NC State defenders into the end zone with him with just over a minute left on the clock. The Pirate defense held one last time as a 49-yard field goal attempt went wide right. As the final whistle sounded, the score was ECU 37, NC State 34. East Carolina finished No. 9 in the postseason poll, its highest ever ranking. Bill Lewis was named AP Coach of the Year. He would resign less than a week later to accept the head coaching position at Georgia Tech.

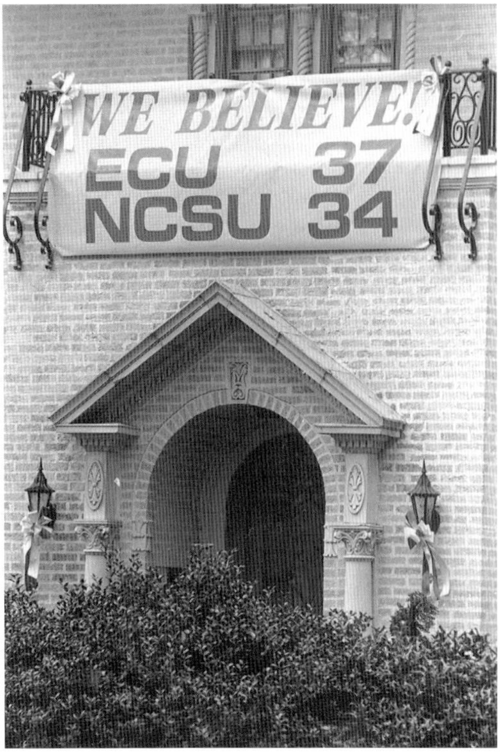

The ECU chancellor's home displays the score of the 1992 Peach Bowl. The "We Believe!" slogan was popularized by Leo Jenkins during the Stasavich era and has been a rallying cry for the Pirates ever since. Many credited the chant with helping start the Peach Bowl comeback.

Wardell "Junior" Smith carries the ball in a 1992 contest. Smith finished his career in 1994 as the all-leading rusher in Pirate history with 3,745 yards. In 1994, he finished in the Top 10 for the Doak Walker Award, presented to the best collegiate running back.

To replace Lewis, athletic director Dave Hart chose Steve Logan. The Oklahoma-born Logan had served as Lewis's offensive coordinator. Logan's first university-level coaching job was at Oklahoma State as a tight ends coach for Jimmy Johnson, the future Dallas Cowboys coach. Logan's only previous head coaching experience was a two-year stint at Hutchinson Community College in Kansas, where he was recognized as the 1982 Kansas Jayhawk Conference Coach of the Year. He then spent time at Tulsa University, the University of Colorado, and Mississippi State in various offensive assistant roles before coming to East Carolina as the running backs coach under Bill Lewis in 1989. Logan implemented a West Coast offensive strategy that featured short, rhythmic passes. His new approach did not catch on initially. A 5-6 season in 1992 was followed by a 2-9 mark in 1993. The lowlight of the 1993 season was the loss of dynamic quarterback Marcus Crandall to a broken leg in the season's second game. Crandall's return, coupled with increased familiarity with Logan's West Coast offensive strategy, propelled the Pirates to a 7-4 regular season finish in 1994.

In 1994, Ron and Mary Ellen Dowdy donated $1 million toward the expansion of Ficklen Stadium. In honor of this gift, the facility was renamed Dowdy-Ficklen Stadium. An additional expansion in 2010 pushed the capacity to 50,000.

The program cover for the 1994 Liberty Bowl is shown here. The Pirates competed in consecutive Liberty Bowls, first losing to Illinois but then defeating Stanford in 1995. Logan took the Pirates to five total bowl games, winning two of them.

David Garrard was a three-year starter for the Pirates at quarterback from 1999 to 2001, never missing a game. In 1999, he led East Carolina to a 9-3 record that included an upset win over the No. 9 Miami Hurricanes at Carter-Finley Stadium. The game was moved to Raleigh due to widespread flooding in eastern North Carolina following Hurricane Floyd. A three-time All-Conference USA selection, Garrard saw ECU play in bowl games each year of his tenure as quarterback. In the 2001 GMAC Bowl, the Pirates lost in double overtime to Marshall, 64-61, in the highest scoring bowl game in NCAA history at that time. Drafted by the Jacksonville Jaguars in 2002, Garrard played 12 seasons in the NFL, where he was named to the 2009 Pro Bowl. In 2013, Garrard was inducted into the ECU Athletics Hall of Fame.

Fans celebrate in Dowdy-Ficklen Stadium during a 2005 contest. The Pirates drew nearly 50,000 purple and gold fans to each home game, where many enjoyed one of the premier tailgating experiences in the nation.

Defensive coordinator Greg Hudson (left) and head coach Skip Holtz celebrate after defeating No. 8 West Virginia in 2008. Holtz coached the Pirates from 2005 to 2009, appearing in four bowl games, with a win in the 2007 Hawaii Bowl. His father was legendary Notre Dame and South Carolina coach Lou Holtz.

East Carolina University hired head coach Ruffin McNeill on January 21, 2010. Affectionately known as "Coach Ruff," he was a defensive back for the Pirates under Pat Dye. From 2000 to 2009, he served as a defensive assistant and assistant head coach at Texas Tech, and acted as the Red Raiders' interim coach for the 2009 Alamo Bowl. At East Carolina, McNeill coached the team to four bowl appearances in his first five seasons, winning the 2013 Beef 'O' Brady's Bowl. McNeill's Pirate teams, noted for their air raid offense, featured four wide receivers and a single running back in an effort to spread out the defense and exploit mismatches. In 2014, wide receiver Justin Hardy set the NCAA all-time receptions record with his 387th catch, besting the mark set by Oklahoma's Ryan Broyles. Hardy was the favored receiver for Pirate quarterback Shane Carden, who set the school record for career passing yards and passing touchdowns in 2014, his senior year. However, 2015 brought a losing season. In December, McNeill was relieved of his duties and a national search for a new head coach was announced.

On December 14, 2015, East Carolina formally announced the hiring of the Pirates' 21st head coach, North Carolina native Scottie Montgomery. Montgomery played wide receiver collegiately at Duke (1996–1999) and professionally for the NFL's Denver Broncos (2000–2002) and Oakland Raiders (2003). He began his coaching career at his alma mater as a wide receivers coach before accepting the same position with the Pittsburgh Steelers under Mike Tomlin. In 2013, he returned to Duke, eventually serving as associate head coach and offensive coordinator. Montgomery directed a balanced offense that in 2014 produced the second-highest season points total in school history and helped the Blue Devils reach three straight bowl games. Pirate Nation welcomes Coach Scottie Montgomery and looks forward to many successful seasons with him at the helm.

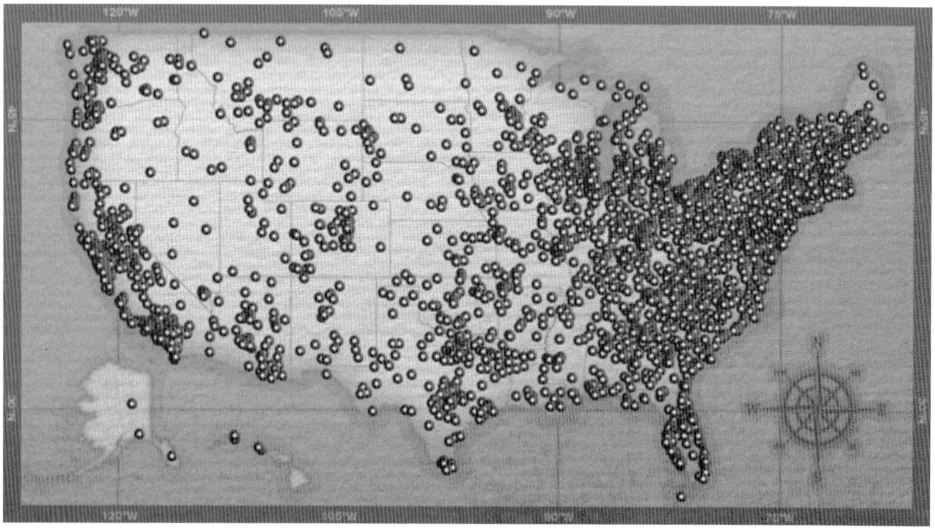